*When a dog runs at you, whistle for him.*

—HENRY DAVID THOREAU (1817–1862)
*American writer*

# THE
# DOG
# LOVER'S
# JOURNAL

## AN ILLUSTRATED
## NOTEBOOK
## WITH QUOTES

*The great pleasure of a dog is that you may make a fool of yourself with him and not only will he not scold you, but will make a fool of himself too.*

—SAMUEL BUTLER (1835–1902)
*English writer*

*. . . every man is a boy when he is with a puppy.*
—HAVILAH BABCOCK (1898–1964)
*American educator and writer*

*There is no doubt that every healthy, normal boy . . . should own a dog at some time in his life, preferably between the ages of forty-five and fifty.*

—ROBERT BENCHLEY (1889–1945)
*American humorist*

*Every puppy should have a boy.*

—ERMA BOMBECK, b. 1927
*American writer*

*She had no particular breed in mind, no unusual requirements. Except the special sense of mutual recognition that tells dog and human they have both come to the right place.*

—LLOYD ALEXANDER, b. 1924
*American writer*

*I like a bit of mongrel myself, whether it's a man or a dog; they're best for everyday.*

—GEORGE BERNARD SHAW (1856–1950)
*British playwright and critic*

*Newfoundland dogs are good to save children from drowning, but you must have a pond of water handy and a child, or else there will be no profit in boarding a Newfoundland.*

—JOSH BILLINGS (1818–1885)
*American humorist*

*Anything as large as a bloodhound or a golden retriever . . . makes a grand hot water bottle.*

—ROGER CARAS, b. 1928
*American writer*

*If manners maketh man, then manner and grooming maketh poodle.*
—JOHN STEINBECK (1902–1968)
*American writer*

*Every dog has his day.*

—MIGUEL DE CERVANTES (1547–1616)
*Spanish writer*

*Acquiring a dog may be the only opportunity a human ever has to choose a relative.*

—MORDECAI SIEGAL
*20th-century American writer*

*Try to see Bob as I see him — a 28-year-old man in a shaggy fur coat who watches television for six hours every evening and never leaves the room for a commercial, if you get my drift.*

—ERMA BOMBECK, b. 1927
*American writer*

*A really companionable and indispensable dog is an accident of nature. You can't get it by breeding for it, and you can't buy it with money. It just happens along.*

—E.B. WHITE (1899–1985)
*American writer*

*There was a slight advantage to being one of the family, for he did not bite the family as often as he bit strangers.*

—JAMES THURBER (1894–1961)
*American writer*

*No man can be condemned for owning a dog. As long as he has a dog he has a friend, and the poorer he gets, the better friend he has.*

—WILL ROGERS (1879–1935)
*American humorist and actor*

*Some dogs are hard to name and some do not seem to need it — they name themselves.*

—ERNEST THOMPSON SETON (1860–1946)
*American writer and naturalist*

*The cryptics name their dogs October, Bennett's aunt, Three Fifteen, Doc Knows, Tuesday, Home Fried, Opus 38, Ask Leslie, and Walter S. Bursley. I make it a point simply to pat these unfortunate dogs on the head, ask no questions, and go about my business.*

—JAMES THURBER (1894–1961)
*American writer*

*It was surely not for nothing that Rover is dog's most common name . . .*

—JOHN GALSWORTHY (1867–1933)
*English novelist and playwright*

*I believe by far the greatest number are owned . . . just for the sheer delight of having a lovely creature round the house to be admired, to admire you, and to keep you company.*

—BARBARA WOODHOUSE, b. 1910
*English dog trainer and writer*

*I have found that when you are deeply troubled, there are things you get from the silent devoted companionship of a dog that you can get from no other source.*

—DORIS DAY, b. 1924
*American actress*

A *man's best friend is his dog.*
    —LORD BYRON (1788–1824)
      *English poet*

*Properly trained, a man can be dog's best friend.*
—CORY FORD (1902–1969)
*American writer*

*The one, absolute, unselfish friend that a man can have in this selfish world, the one that never deserts him, the one that never proves ungrateful or treacherous, is his dog.*

—GEORGE GRAHAM VEST (1830–1904)
*American politician*

*If you pick up a starving dog and make him prosperous, he will not bite you. This is the principal difference between a dog and a man.*

—MARK TWAIN (1835–1910)
*American writer*

*The plain fact that my dog loves me more than I love him is undeniable and always fills one with a certain amount of shame.*

— KONRAD LORENZ, b. 1903
*Austrian zoologist and writer*

*You've seen that look. The way a young painter looks at a Rembrandt or Titian. The way Liz Taylor looks at Richard Burton. The way Zsa Zsa looks at mink. That's how a poodle looks at its master.*

—JACQUELINE SUSANN (1921–1974)
*American writer*

*The dog was cold and in pain. But being only a dog it did not occur to him to trot off home to the comfort of the library fire and leave his master to fend for himself.*

—ALBERT PAYSON TERHUNE (1872–1942)
*American writer*

*. . . the dog who meets with a good master is the happier of the two.*

—MAURICE MAETERLINCK (1862–1949)
*Belgian poet and playwright*

*A man can do worse sometimes than follow a tip his dog gives him.*

—ALBERT PAYSON TERHUNE (1872–1942)
*American writer*

*Try it on the dog.*

—MARK TWAIN (1835–1910)
*American writer*

*When a man's dog turns against him, it is time for a wife to pack her trunk and go home to mama.*

—MARK TWAIN (1835–1910)
*American writer*

*To his dog, every man is Napoleon; hence the constant popularity of dogs.*

—ALDOUS HUXLEY (1894–1963)
*English writer*

*Your dog is your only philosopher.*

—PLATO (c. 427–348 B.C.)
*Greek philosopher*

*I myself have known some very profoundly thoughtful dogs.*

—JAMES THURBER (1894–1961)
*American writer*

*I've seen a look in dogs' eyes, a quickly vanishing look of amazed contempt, and I am convinced that basically dogs think humans are nuts.*

—JOHN STEINBECK (1902–1968)
*American writer*

*Mad dogs and Englishmen go out in the midday sun.*
—NOEL COWARD (1899–1963)
*English actor and playwright*

*A dog, more than any other creature, it seems to me, gets interested in one subject, theme, or object, in life, and pursues it with a fixity of purpose which would be inspiring to Man if it weren't so troublesome.*

—E.B. WHITE (1899–1985)
*American writer*

*Owing to the artificially complex life led by city dogs of the present day, they tend to lose the simple systems of intuition which once guided all breeds, and frequently lapse into what comes very close to mental perplexity.*

—JAMES THURBER (1894–1961)
*American writer*

*Dogs laugh, but they laugh with their tails.*
—MAX EASTMAN (1883–1969)
*American editor and writer*

*Those sighs of a dog! They go to the heart so much more deeply than the sighs of our own kind because they are utterly unintended, regardless of effect, emerging from one who, heaving them, knows not that they have escaped him!*

— JOHN GALSWORTHY (1867–1933)
*English writer*

*Charley likes to get up early, and he likes me to get up early too. And why shouldn't he? Right after his breakfast he goes back to sleep.*

—JOHN STEINBECK    (1902–1968)
*American writer*

*It's not for nothing that good dogs don't wear watches. They're on dog time, which seems the best time of all.*

—JOE MURRAY
*20th-century American writer*

*It's obvious that people expect vets to have well-trained dogs — unfortunately, Bodie is unaware of this fact.*

—JAMES HERRIOT, b. 1916
*British veterinarian and writer*

*Can't learn an old dog new tricks.*
—MARK TWAIN (1835–1910)
*American writer*

*. . . a door is what a dog is perpetually on the wrong side of.*
—OGDEN NASH (1902–1971)
*American writer*

*Anyone who hates dogs and children can't be all bad.*

*If dogs could talk, perhaps we'd find it just as hard to get along with them as we do with people.*

—KAREL CAPEK (1890–1938)
*Czech journalist*

The nose of the bulldog has been slanted backwards so that he can breathe without letting go.

—WINSTON S. CHURCHILL (1874–1965)
*British statesman and writer*

*A dog likes to obey. It gives them security.*

—JAMES HERRIOT, b. 1916
*British veterinarian and writer*

*To a man the greatest blessing is individual liberty; to a dog is the last word in despair.*

—WILLIAM LYON PHELPS (1865–1943)
*American educator and critic*

*I would rather train a striped zebra to balance an Indian club than induce a dachshund to heed my slightest command.*

—E.B. WHITE (1899–1985)
*American writer*

*I was one of the luckier women who came to motherhood with some experience. I owned a Yorkshire terrier for three years.*

—ERMA BOMBECK, b. 1927
*American writer*

*Barking dogs seldom bite.*

—NATHAN BAILEY, d. 1742
*English lexicographer*

*A bargain dog never bites.*
—OGDEN NASH (1902–1971)
*American writer*

*There are several reasons humans and dogs can communicate so comfortably. One...is that...dogs train their owners to respond to particular signals.*

—KAROL RICE
*20th-century American writer*

*Dogs are usually left cold by all phases of psychology, mental telepathy, and the like.*

—JAMES THURBER (1894–1961)
*American writer*

*Ever consider what they must think of us? I mean, here we come back
from the grocery store with the most amazing haul — chicken, pork,
half a cow . . . They must think we're the greatest hunters on earth!*

—ANNE TYLER, b. 1941
*American writer*

*For many dogs, begging is a full-time job.*

—CAROLE LEA BENJAMIN
*20th-century American writer*

*Every dog is a lion at home.*
—PROVERB

*Every dog should have a man of his own. There is nothing like a well-behaved person around the house to spread the dog's blanket for him or bring him his supper when he comes home man-tired at night.*

—CORY FORD (1902–1969)
*American writer*

*The ad in the paper said "puppy, partially housebroken." That is like being partially pregnant.*

—ERMA BOMBECK, b. 1927
*American writer*

*Anybody who doesn't know what soap tastes like never washed a dog.*
—FRANKLIN P. JONES (1905–1975)
*American writer*

*A dog is like an eternal Peter Pan, a child who never grows old and who therefore is always available to love and be loved.*

—AARON KATCHER, b. 1932
*American educator and psychiatrist*

*Dogs' lives are too short. Their only fault really.*

—AGNES SLIGH TURNBULL (1888–1982)
*American writer*

... *a boy and a dog should grow up together, making their own*
*mistakes and discoveries, each molding himself to the other.*

—HAVILAH BABCOCK (1898–1964)
*American educator and writer*

*A dog teaches a boy fidelity, perseverance, and to turn around three times before lying down.*

—ROBERT BENCHLEY (1889–1945)
*American humorist*

*It was Vixen's custom . . . to sleep in my bed, her head on the pillow like a Christian; and when morning came I would always find that the little thing had braced her feet against the wall and pushed me to the very edge of the cot.*

—RUDYARD KIPLING (1865–1936)
*English writer*

*We had been lost without a dog in the house, and it was a great relief to have filled that awful gap. . . . Helen had a dog to feed again and I had a companion in my car and on my nightly walks. . . .*

—JAMES HERRIOT, b. 1916
*British veterinarian and writer*

*One of the animals which a generous and sociable man would soonest become is a dog.*

—LEIGH HUNT (1784–1859)
*English writer*

*Love me, love my dog.*

—JOHN HEYWOOD (1497–1580)
*English poet*

*A dog, particularly an exotic like Charley, is a bond between strangers.*
*Many conversations en route began with "What degree of dog is that?"*

—JOHN STEINBECK (1902–1968)
*American writer*

*Small puppies are rather like wrinkled sausages. They are all stomach and, in the case of bloodhounds, ears.*

—ROGER CARAS, b. 1928
*American writer*

A dog is a man's best friend.
He has a tail on one end.
Up in front he has teeth
And four legs underneath.

—OGDEN NASH (1902–1971)
*American writer*

*The devotion of the dog has been greatly exaggerated. What a dog really wants is excitement. He is easily bored, cannot amuse himself, and therefore demands entertainment. The dog's ideal is a life of active uselessness.*

—WILLIAM LYON PHELPS (1865–1943)
*American educator and critic*

*Probably no one man should have as many dogs in his life
as I have had...*

—JAMES THURBER (1894–1961)
*American writer*

*Nobody ever sold eleven puppies before noon on Sunday.*
—EILEEN SCHROEDER
*20th-century American writer*

*. . . my husband convinced me the children would grow up to steal hubcaps without the security and affection of a dog.*

—ERMA BOMBECK, b. 1927
*American writer*

*Dachshunds are ideal dogs for small children, as they are already stretched and pulled to such a length that the child cannot do much harm one way or the other.*

—ROBERT BENCHLEY (1889–1945)
*American humorist*

*I was unlucky in having a dogless childhood. My mother belonged to the generation which had just discovered bacteria . . .*

— KONRAD LORENZ, b. 1903
*Austrian zoologist and writer*

*The best way to get a puppy is to beg for a baby brother — and they'll settle for a puppy every time.*

—WINSTON PENDELTON, b. 1910
*American writer*

*He had a way of taking Buck's head roughly between his hands, and resting his own head upon Buck's, of shaking him back and forth, the while calling him ill names that to Buck were love names.*

—JACK LONDON (1876–1916)
*American writer*

*. . . being patted is what it is all about.*

—ROGER CARAS, b. 1928
*American writer*

It was the dream of every canine to someday live out where every dog had his own tree . . . and where fleas had to register at the city limits and carry their I.D.s at all times.

—ERMA BOMBECK, b. 1927
*American writer*

*The old dog barks backwards without getting up.*
*I can remember when he was a pup.*

—ROBERT FROST (1874–1963)
*American poet*

*. . . not Carnegie, Vanderbilt and Astor together could have raised money enough to buy a quarter share in my little dog. . .*

—ERNEST THOMPSON SETON (1860–1946)
*American writer and naturalist*

*Dogs are as important to me as people.*

—DORIS DAY, b. 1924
*American actress*

*The one best place to bury a good dog is in the heart of his master.*

—BEN HUR LAMPMAN (1886–1954)
*American writer*

*Cave Canem*
*(Beware of the Dog)*

—Epitaph on the gravestone of James Thurber's dog, Muggs

*Ask a man about his dog and you have his heart.*
—FERN MICHAELS *(Roberta Anderson, b. 1942; Mary Kuczkir, b. 1933)*
    *American writers*

*Nor does anyone who ever owned a dog need to be told the sound a man makes as he bends over a dog that has been his for many years . . .*

—ERIC KNIGHT (1897–1943)
*American writer and drama critic*

*It is a strange thing, love. Nothing but love has made the dog lose his wild freedom, to become the servant of man.*

—D.H. LAWRENCE (1885–1930)
*English writer*

*A dog is the only thing on this earth that loves you more than he loves himself.*

—JOSH BILLINGS (1818–1885)
*American humorist*

*My little old dog:*
*A heart beat at my feet.*

—EDITH WHARTON (1862–1937)
*American writer*